TLC

Teams, Leaders, and Change
TLC: Accelerating Women in Leadership

Workbook

Dr. Amanda Goodson
Dr. Yvette Rice
Odetta Scott, MBA, MSOD

AMANDA GOODSON

Edited by LLVE, LLC: Dr. Yvette Rice
Typesetting by Inktobook.com
Published by Amanda Goodson Global, LLC

Printed in the U.S.A.

Paperback ISBN: 978-951501-27-3
eBook ISBN: 978-951501-28-0

Table of Contents

It is Time, Again!

The Teams, Leaders, and Change: Accelerating Women in Leadership Workbook was written to coincide with the *TLC: Teams, Leaders, and Change: Accelerating Women in Leadership* book. Continuing our vision for our TLC: Teams, Leaders, and Change: Accelerating Women in STEM program that was birthed when we were together in Washington D.C., at the BEYA STEM Global Competitive Conference in February 2020, we knew it was time to expand our vision to all women seeking to expand their leadership footprint.

There is evidence that shows that "Fortune 500 companies experienced a return on investment of 66% in invested capital, a 42% increase in sales, and return on equity increases averaging 53% when there were three or more women in directorship positions in their companies relative to those companies with fewer women directors."[1] It's no accident that gender-diverse companies are more likely to outperform non-gender diverse companies by 15 percent, while ethnically diverse companies are more likely to outperform less ethnically diverse companies by 35 percent.[2] Even though these statistics support the importance of Diversity, Equity, and Inclusion in the marketplace, a vast number of women professionals continue to be excluded from leadership seats at the table. Whether these deficits are based on intentional exclusion resulting from gender bias, double standards in the marketplace, gender stereotypes, or extreme work schedules that discourage women from competing for management roles, there is a distinct gender gap relative to career women and executive leadership.[3] Because of these inequalities for women in the marketplace, we at WeTECH Rocks believe *"It is Time, Again!"*

We asked ourselves, "What can we do together to become a global leader in bridging the gap for not just women in STEM (science, technology, engineering, and mathematics), but also for the

---

1   Anita Borg, "The Case for Investing in Women," Retrieved from https://www.theneweconomy.com/business/anita-borg-report-makes-strong-case-for-investingin-women. April 9, 2014.
2   McKinsey & Company, "Why Diversity Matters," Vivian Hunt, Dennis Layton, and Sara Prince, January 2015.
3   Marshall Swafford and Ryan Anderson, "Addressing the Gender Gap: Women's Perceived Barriers to Pursuing STEM Careers," (Vol. 4, No. 1). Journal of Research in Technical Careers. 63–64. http://dx.doi.org/10.9741/2578-2118.1070, May 2020.

advancement of women in leadership in the marketplace in any industry?" Glassdoor, a website where individuals seek employment and current and former employees anonymously review companies, states that 67 percent of job seekers believe diversity is a vital factor when evaluating companies and job offers.[4] It's not unusual for prospective employees, when examining a company, to look at the organization online and then shy away when they look at the leaders of that company and see no diversity in the executive staff. However, consider that the woman reading our book and workbook might become the person who breaks that barrier. There may be a purpose for her to be there. Instead of drawing back in fear of being overlooked or undervalued, it could be an opportunity for her to break that glass.

We believe it is time for ladies to not just stand up, but to stand out and be heard in every industry. We are not done yet. We are not there yet. It is imperative for women to look at what they can do, as opposed to what they have been told they can do, and then take their place to do mighty things as professionals.

It is time for us as women to have a *voice* and *dignity* in the marketplace through how we communicate, how we share, and how we lead to shift workplace culture.

It is time to bring hope and encouragement for those women already in the marketplace to burn the light even *brighter* for women who aspire to what they have already achieved.

In this workbook, we deliver the five principles defined in our book, *TLC: Teams, Leaders, and Change: Accelerating Women in Leadership*. We challenge you to take the time to complete the exercises in the workbook to help you become a catalyst to the TLC (teams, leaders, and change) you will *perpetuate* as a woman in leadership in your various industries—while giving yourself the TLC (tender loving care) you need to *go forward* as a bold, confident, woman impacting the marketplace and workplace culture.

---

4   Glassdoor Inc. blog, November 17, 2014.

1

Identify your style, exploit your strengths, and recognize your differences to manage them well.

Leaders may be bold, or they may be deep and analytical. There are other leaders who are gregarious, animated, and strong at developing relationships—and then there are those who are positive and may have an upbeat mantra for each day: Magnificent Monday, Terrific Tuesday, Wonderful Wednesday, Thankful Thursday, and Fantastic Friday.

What kind of leader are you? Or, are you yet to come to the realization that you are a leader? Is a title necessary to be a leader? Can you learn to lead from any chair by developing your skills to influence? Influencers are willing to *learn*, *listen* to others who have gone before them, and are willing to *stretch* themselves. They also surround themselves with people as good as, or better than, they are. As you are authentic to your true self and learn how to be an influencer, you can get in the room, get to the table, and make an impact.

How you show up daily and interact with people will provide direction to how you execute, inspire, and strategize in a business setting. Are you strong? Are you communicative? Are you detailed? Attributes that can define your leadership style include defined focus areas such as strategy, continuous improvement, and talent development, with each role infused by a passion and energy to make a difference.

TLC EXERCISE

This exercise will help you understand your realized and unrealized strengths and characteristics, how you feel, think, and behave, and how you produce actions and behaviors from others. Why is it important? It is important to exploit your strengths and augment your differences in order to be able to manage yourself in any other way. This is a foundational piece of who you are. Not knowing who you are, how you interact with others, and how you communicate, makes it more difficult for you to be a part of a higher productive team and to lead change.

What is Identifying Your Style, Exploiting Your Strengths, and Recognizing Your Differences in Order to Manage Them Well?

To identify your style, exploit your strengths and recognize your differences to be able to manage them well, the following steps should be identified and taken.

Answer the following Questions.

The first question allows you to list your "productive ways of being" to identify how you act and what you produce that adds value to others. The second question causes you to ascertain your "nonvalue-added ways of being" by honestly evaluating areas where your attitude or actions do not add value to those around you. The third question reveals what others have noticed about you all your life.

- **"What are the things I am doing today that I like the most?"**

_____

_____

_____

_____

_____

_____

- **"What are the things I least like to do?"**

_____

_____

_____

_____

_____

_____

_____

- **"If I were to go to my stakeholders—those who know me well such as my spouse, parents, siblings, classmates, and co-workers—what will they say I do well or don't do well?"**

_____

_____

_____

_____

_____

_____

_____

SELF-AWARENESS QUOTES

Debbie Ford: Premier Author, New York Times best-selling author, and an internationally recognized expert in the field of personal transformation and human potential

"Self-awareness is the ability to take an honest look at your life without any attachment to it being right or wrong, good or bad."

Daniel Goleman: Premier Author, Leading Expert on Emotional Intelligence

"If your emotional abilities aren't in hand, if you don't have self-awareness, if you are not able to manage your distressing emotions, if you can't have empathy and have effective relationships, then no matter how smart you are, you are not going to get very far."

Lawrence Bossidy: Former CEO Allied Signal/Businessman

"Self-awareness gives you the capacity to learn from your mistakes as well as your successes. It enables you to keep growing."

Develop Your *SAS!*

S: SELF
A: AWARENESS
S: STRENGTH

Perform a SPOT analysis on Yourself. Honestly identify and rate the following areas in your life professionally and personally.

The **SPOT** analysis takes what you learned about your "productive ways of being" and "nonvalue-added ways of being" to look at yourself from the standpoint of your **s**trengths, **p**otential areas for improvement, **o**pportunities, and **t**hreats.

- **S**trengths represent areas where you believe you are most effective and therefore place you in a position of advantage. These identify things you can *leverage*.

- **P**otential areas for improvement can come from places where you feel you are at a disadvantage and, therefore, need more training or development. You can take a class or read a book and *learn* how to address these areas.

- **O**pportunities constitute areas that you believe you can exploit to even greater advantage. *Listen* to others and strive to apply and make the most of what they tell you.

- **T**hreats are elements, usually external, that can damage or even endanger your ability to fulfill your mission. As you recognize these, your job is to lessen them.

Fill in each quadrant using the guidelines established above.

SPOT Analysis	
Strengths	**P**otential areas for improvement
1.	1.
2.	2.
3.	3.
4.	4.
5.	5.
Opportunities	**T**hreats
1.	1.
2.	2.
3.	3.
4.	4.
5.	5.

Take an Agile EQ™ (Emotion Intelligence) Assessment to learn how to successfully interact with colleagues.

Several assessments (such as Everything DiSC®) can help you discover your various attributes. One of those attributes is your emotional intelligence. The capacity to be aware of, control, and express your emotions in interpersonal relationships with others is called "emotional intelligence,"—and it is vital to effective leadership.

Daniel Goleman is an expert on emotional intelligence, as well as an internationally known psychologist and lecturer. He says there are six styles of leadership. "Coercive leaders demand immediate compliance. Authoritative leaders mobilize people toward a vision. Affiliative leaders create emotional bonds and harmony. Democratic leaders build consensus through participation. Pacesetting leaders expect excellence and self-direction. And coaching leaders develop people for the future."[1] Meanwhile, the four attributes of emotional intelligence are self-awareness, self-management, social and situational awareness, and relationship management. The ability to understand yourself and your emotional intelligence as it pertains to your leadership attributes and style will help you flex when you need to adjust to get others galvanized and engaged.

Dr. Amanda Goodson (WeTECH Rocks) is licensed by John Wiley & Sons, Inc. to assist you in obtaining an *Everything DiSC® Agile EQ™*[2]. The Agile EQ™ assessment will help you learn how to choose the most effective response when engaging with others in complex interactions.

When you pull together a team as a leader, working together with them to leverage their differences and exploit their strengths is very important. Once you understand the differences and strengths, you create a capability for yourself, your team, and your organization that will propel it forward in ways you never thought possible.

There will be times as a leader when you feel hesitant about saying, "I don't know," or "I want help." You may think of it as a sign of weakness if you have to ask someone else for answers. It is not. Don't allow yourself to be put in a spot where you feel like you can't reach out to someone to gain knowledge or perspective. Instead, strive to be a self-aware leader who knows where you may not be as strong and surround yourself with people who are stronger in those areas than you. That will accelerate the team to move forward because every base is covered, and you will end up receiving the best of the best in every strength to be more efficient, effective, and high performing as a team.

Use the Action Plan Template provided to identify your Focus Areas based on the SPOT analysis you completed. Carefully describe actions you plan to take to address potential areas of improvement and opportunities. Indicate how you plan to lessen the threats you identified in your SPOT analysis. Additionally, discuss how you will exploit your strengths.

---

1   Daniel Goleman, "Leadership That Gets Results," (Harvard Business Review Classics). Harvard Business School Publishing Corporation, 2017.
2   John Wiley & Sons, Inc.

IDENTIFY YOUR STYLE: SELF-AWARENESS			
ACTION PLAN TEMPLATE			
IDENTIFY YOUR FOCUS AREAS			
Strengths	Potential Areas for Improvement	Opportunities	Threats
Enter characteristic you want to focus on from the above (SPOT analysis)			
Action Item	Task Description		Due Date
Action 1			
Action 2			
Action 3			
Action 4			
Action 5			
Action 6			
Action 7			
Action 8			
Action 9			
Action 10			
I am committed to developing my SAS Self-Awareness Strength!	Participant Signature: _____ Date:		

When dealing with conflict, there are differences in opinions, values, and skills that pull in strong emotions and trigger behaviors. Therefore, if you don't deal with conflict well, you may need to have a conflict analysis done to find out how you can better handle conflict and identify ways you can improve.

A great way to mitigate conflict is to employ the five functions of a team required for conflict management developed by Dr. Rice and discussed in our book, *TLC: Teams, Leaders, and Change: Accelerating Women in Leadership*. Just use a little **GRACE**™:

G	Good vibes and trust. You are there for each other and those you serve.
R	Recognition of each team member that produces a healthy respect for others' opinions different from your own.
A	Accountability and maintaining a sense of responsibility. You must do your part without judging your teammates.
C	Character. Your character exemplifies who you are as you fulfill your purpose on the earth.
E	Excellence. Your work must always be excellent.

If you are going into a new environment, you will be promoting yourself into a place that resonates with your goals by virtue of **GRACE**. Identify the foundational pieces of who you are and how each area of your **SPOT** analysis resonates with where you are in your current situation and in your future state.

1. _____

2. _____

3. _____

4. _____

5. _____

6. _____

7. _____

List how you communicate and interact with others.

1. _____

2. _____

3. _____

4. _____

5. _____

6. _____

Are you focused and detail-oriented? Give three (3) examples of areas where your focus and detail orientation are required.

1. _____

2. _____

3. _____

2

Communicate and connect early and often by speaking up and speaking out in professional meetings and by using technical writing to create excellence and advance your career.

As stated in the TLC book, communication happens in two ways: verbal and nonverbal. Verbal communication includes your tone of voice and the words that you speak. Nonverbal communication involves body language, hand motions, eye contact, and facial expressions, all of which modify what you are communicating. In fact, listeners will not only hear what we say, but how we say it. Often, we are not aware of how much nonverbal communication informs how credible we come across and whether or not what we say really matters to those who are listening.

That established, the person you communicate with the most is yourself. Whether you realize it or not, you can paint a defeated picture of yourself in the marketplace when you tell yourself you're not good enough or smart enough—especially as a woman.

Katty Kay and Claire Shipman expose the gender confidence gap in their book, *The Confidence Code*. Their research reveals that even women at the top of their professions still question their worth, saying they were "just lucky" or that they somehow "slid through" or feel like a "fraud." Furthermore, they state that, while women tend to underestimate their abilities, men overestimate theirs by 30 percent. Our communication and how we first speak to ourselves can be detrimental to our ability to succeed.

WHAT CAN YOU DO TO IMPROVE YOUR SELF-TALK?

Before communicating with anyone else, you must learn to communicate positively with yourself. You must defeat any negative voices by learning to develop the right self-talk. Former First Lady of the United States, Eleanor Roosevelt, has been quoted as saying, "No one can make you feel inferior without your consent." As women, we cannot give consent to that negative voice that reinforces our insecurity or inferiority. Why? There will be times others will not see the greatness in you; therefore, you must learn to encourage yourself through positive confession.

You Were Fearfully and Wonderfully Made!

TLC EXERCISE

Identify and list three (3) negative statements you speak or think about yourself regularly. Remember, we can hear our thoughts! Thus, you are communicating to yourself.

1. _____

2. _____

3. _____

Now, commit to audibly speaking these positive **"I Am"** statements about yourself daily for the next three weeks. Note how you feel each day after making these confessions.

1.	**I am fearfully and wonderfully made, and I am in the marketplace, in my organization at this time for a purpose.**
2.	**I am intelligent, gifted, and capable of successfully completing any task set before me.**
3.	**I am beautiful inside and out. I am one of a kind. I was placed on this earth to leave my own mark to make the world a better place with my unique fingerprints.**

Putting these confessions in front of you on the wall or on a mirror while you are getting dressed in the morning allows you to speak positive things to yourself. There is a word of wisdom that states, "Out of the fullness of the heart the mouth speaks… Overwhelming feeling will express itself in speech; originally with biblical allusion to Matthew 12:34…The saying is recorded from the late 14th century.[1] By creating a habit of speaking positively about yourself, you will eliminate those negative statements from your thoughts.

WHY IS HOW WE COMMUNICATE ESSENTIAL?

Your communication style and how you communicate orally and in writing are essential to advancing your career. In today's environment, organizations look for people possessing a total package in terms of verbal and written communication. This, augmented by being a technical writer to create excellence and advance your career, demonstrates that you are serious and promotable to the organization.

How well you communicate will also affect your ability to lead. For example, succinctly communicating an organization's vision is critical. If we cannot express ourselves in a way that generates passion within our teams relative to the vision, we'll upset the direction of the organization.

WHAT DO YOU NEED TO DO, AND/OR WHAT STEPS SHOULD YOU TAKE TO IMPROVE YOUR COMMUNICATION SKILLS?

To create energy around yourself, understand your tone of voice and look at your body language. This gives others, whether it be your customers or other business professionals, a sense of who you are.

TLC EXERCISE

Identify and list three (3) ways that your communication style can promote the value you want to bring to your organization.

1. _____

2. _____

3. _____

Identify and list three (3) ways you demonstrate you are listening first, before speaking.

1. _____

2. _____

3. _____

---

1 Oxford Reference, Oxford University Press, Copyrighted © 2022. All rights reserved. https://www.oxfordreference.com/view/10.1093/oi/authority.20110803095838418.

Identify and list three (3) ways your body language, which should match the words coming out of your mouth, equals the personal presence that people want to learn from.

1. _____

2. _____

3. _____

Identify and list three (3) ways that you openly and honestly communicate with your team without judgment.

1. _____

2. _____

3. _____

Identify and list three (3) ways that you clearly communicate gratitude and appreciation with your organization.

1. _____

2. _____

3. _____

Utilizing your **SPOT** analysis from Chapter 1 and assuming positive intent from the standpoint of how you can grow and best connect and act upon your discernment, describe when you have had to use this scenario. Document the outcome.

1. _____

2. _____

3. _____

4. _____

5. _____

Describe how **GRACE** can be used to communicate more effectively.

1. _____

2. _____

3. _____

4. _____

5. _____

ACTION ACTIVITIES

1. Record a 2-minute video of yourself. Listen to how you sound, observe your verbal and non-verbal communications, and notice whether or not this demonstrates who you are becoming.

    1. _____

    2. _____

    3. _____

2. Draft a business memo to a leader two (2) levels up. (Scenario to be provided by the facilitator)

_____

_____

_____

_____

_____

Strive to be great!

It's already been mentioned in our book, *Teams, Leaders, and Change TLC: Accelerating Women in Leadership*, but it can't be repeated enough: you bring something to the table. You have a body of knowledge that other people don't. As you innovate, create, and leverage who you are, realize that you are needed. Please do not make light of that fact.

The greatness in you requires that you exude confidence in yourself and what you offer. There is a difference between being assertive and being aggressive. Assertiveness is strength under control. Aggressiveness is strength without control. Let's say there's a woman in a room of male leaders having a conversation. She possesses more knowledge in a certain area than the others, yet one of her colleagues keeps challenging her. A woman with strength under control will listen to everyone's feedback to the degree to which it is appropriate and then thank them for their comments. Then she can articulately communicate her area of expertise without being aggressive. She will do so with a cool, calm, confident tone of voice.

However, a woman who has strength without control will react. "What do you mean by that? I am the one that knows this. I am the expert!" Her voice gets louder, her inflection is raised, and she tries to shut everyone down. Later, those in the meeting will think she was angry, but she wasn't. She was passionate, but that passion had driven her to the point where she was not in control. The constant challenges to her knowledge and authority were the trigger.

An aggressive woman can be perceived as attacking, threatening, and disrespectful. An assertive woman stands up for herself or her views by being controlled and respectful, effectively connecting and communicating in a way where her self-value is equal to how she values others.

WHAT IS STRIVING TO BE GREAT?

Greatness speaks to constant and never-ending improvement. Being great starts on the inside. It is how you see yourself, how you show up in the room, and the conversation you have with yourself.

Striving to be great requires exuding confidence in yourself, knowing what you offer, and knowing your capabilities. It also means you can be assertive without being aggressive.

WHY IS IT IMPORTANT?

You must see yourself as great before anyone else does. Have an accelerated conversation with yourself before coming into the room to have more confidence. Having the conversation before coming into the room allows you to lean in and actively accept challenges, and become great from the inside out.

WHAT DO YOU NEED TO DO?

Remember our discussion in Chapter 2 regarding positive communication and the right self-talk? Remove all negative talk from your mind before entering the room by accelerating the conversation within yourself to match who you are becoming.

TLC EXERCISE

Greatness speaks to constant and never-ending improvement. Referencing the story of the caterpillar in our book, Teams, Leaders, and Change TLC: Accelerating Women in Leadership, on pages 27 – 28, determine how you can be great by leveraging this story. List three (3) to five (5) points that speak to your scenario for never-ending improvement (i.e., things you want to do better).

1. _____

2. _____

3. _____

4. _____

5. _____

To create a discipline that will take you to greatness, ask yourself Amanda's six "P's."

- **Passion:** Can I love it? Can it give me lift?
- **People:** Will people around me notice it, ask about it, and even pay for it?
- **Preparation:** Am I willing to get the education, experience, and exposure to develop and maximize it?
- **Position:** Will I put the time and effort in to set goals; and then deconstruct those goals into objectives to achieve them?

- **Purpose:** Am I driven toward that place, knowing why it is important and certain that my heart knows it is right for me?
- **Proclivity:** Am I bent or inclined to lean that way?

Responding to your answers to Amanda's six "P's" and utilizing your SPOT analysis created in Chapter 1, reflect on your strategy for becoming greater.

1. _____

2. _____

3. _____

4. _____

5. _____

Examine the different stages of transforming from a caterpillar to becoming a butterfly you previously read. Make a comparison of the various stages of metamorphosis to determine how greatness starts to emerge. Then, utilizing this comparison, describe where you are now in your career and how you can expect to move to the next level, understanding that at each new level, the metamorphosis process continues.

_____

_____

_____

_____

_____

_____

_____

Use strategic planning, which is foundational and critical to map your future.

As a leader in the marketplace, you can achieve outcomes that will cause you as a woman in leadership to grow, mature, and excel over a long-term period by using strategic planning. An essential method WeTECH recommends to move from your current state to a desired future state is reverse planning via GAP analysis. A tried and true tool, you can use GAP analysis to determine what steps need to be taken to map your future by doing the following:

1. List characteristic factors (such as competencies and performance levels) of the present situation or "what is."

_____

_____

_____

_____

2. List factors needed to achieve future objectives or "what should be."

_____

_____

_____

3. Highlight the gaps that exist between the "what is" and "what should be" that need to be filled to achieve your future objectives.

_____

_____

_____

_____

WHY IS STRATEGIC PLANNING IMPORTANT?

A strategic plan is imperative to your progress. If there is no roadmap, any road taken will get you somewhere, but not necessarily to the preferred destination. The strategic plan enhances your control and contributes to improved performance, and when combined with the GAP analysis, it leads to succession planning and a future pipeline for growth.

HOW IS REVERSE PLANNING BENEFICIAL TO MOVING YOU FORWARD WITH A STRATEGIC PLAN?

To better understand reverse planning, think of how a GPS works. When we enter the address of our destination into the system, the GPS works backward to find the most direct route to where we want to go. It starts at the endpoint and progresses back toward the starting point. In doing so, it analyzes the trip by identifying obstacles along the way such as road construction or closures, estimating how long it'll take to get there depending on how much traffic might exist, and coming up with a street-by-street path we can follow and rely upon to complete the trip successfully. Then, because of its reverse planning, we drive onward to move forward toward the destination.

Indeed, hindsight is always 20/20. If you have already been there, you will know the steps to get there. That's one of the things that makes reverse planning so powerful and effective.

WHAT DO YOU NEED TO DO?

Utilization of the GAP analysis methodologies provides the direction for taking you to your destination by filling in the performance gaps and allowing you to approach the plan from the beginning and then work your way forward. The reverse planning methodology enables you to see where you have been, where you are going, and then provides an avenue for achieving success again.

We can even use the GPS example to explain another benefit of reverse GAP analysis. As we're driving, sometimes something will come up that'll force us to deviate from the path the GPS planned out for us. It might be something necessary, such as a quick errand. It could be accidental, such as not merging safely over from the left lane when we needed to turn right, forcing us to backtrack. It may be as simple as a spur-of-the-moment choice to take another road for part of the journey because we liked the view it provided. Whatever it was, the GPS recalibrated to get us back on the correct route and keep us there.

In the same way, you will have some detours along the journey to your desired future. The beauty of reverse planning is that it is flexible. It is revisited and adjusted on a quarterly, monthly, even weekly basis, but always in such a way as to keep you headed in the right direction toward the manifestation of your future reality.

WHAT IS FRESH WILL™?

The first letters of each characteristic of Amanda's acronym FRESH WILL™ create a fresh, renewed purpose to your life that gives you direction and propels you forward. It takes you from your current reality to your future reality and reignites your passion so that you can make a declaration to live out your FRESH WILL™ and manifest outcomes that bring your future reality to fruition.

Finances
Relationships
Energy
Spirituality
Health
Work
Innovation
Leisure
Long Life

TLC EXERCISE

Referring to page 36 of our book, *Teams, Leaders, and Change TLC: Accelerating Women in Leadership*, list the gaps relative to your life and career in light of Amanda's nine **Fresh Will**™ characteristics of her **Goodson 9-Block©**.

Finances	Relationships	Energy
Spirituality	Health	Work
Innovation	Leisure	Long Life

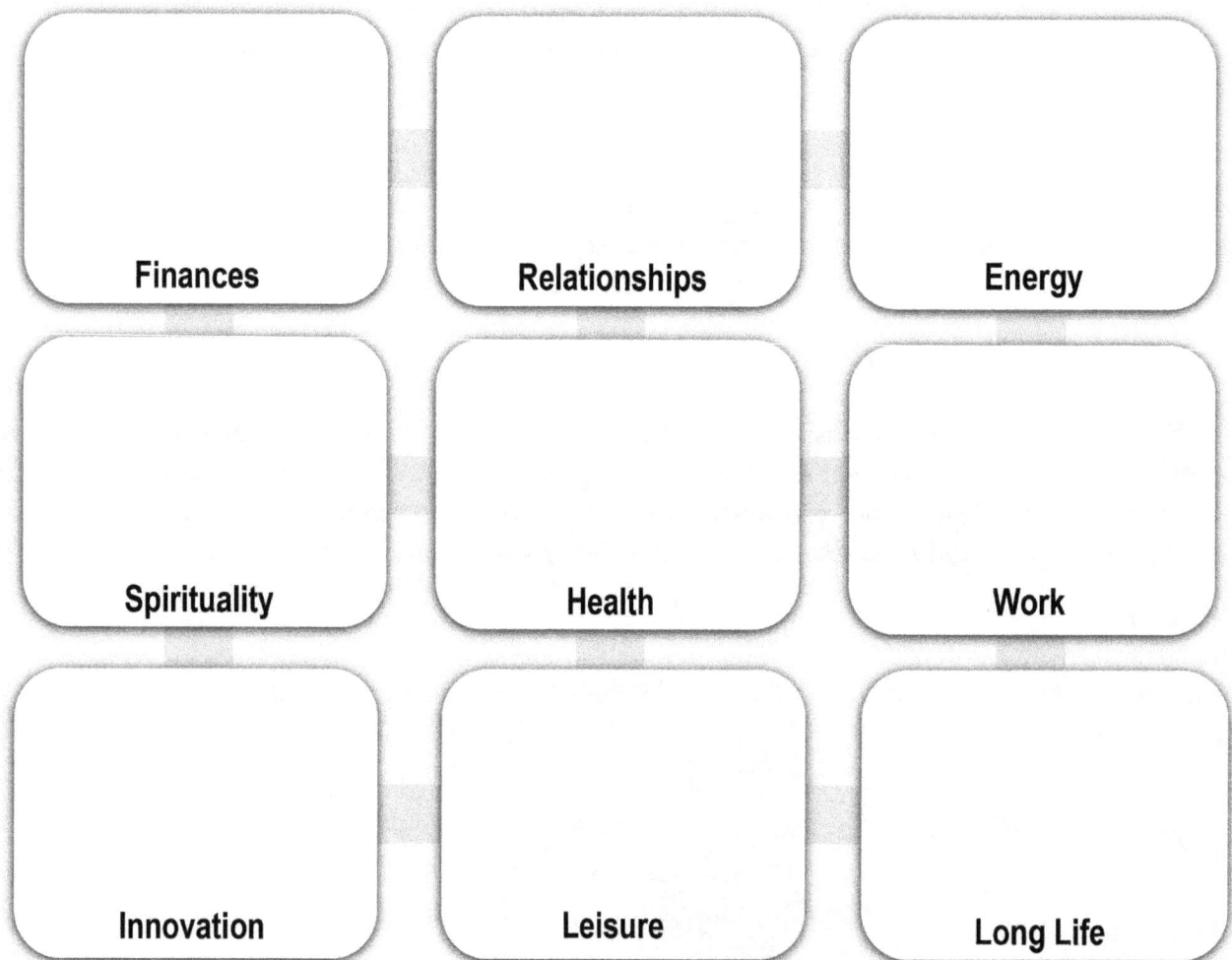

**Goodson Affirmation 9-Block™ AGG 2018 – This cannot be
duplicated without the written consent of the author.**

As we look at strategy, your strategy should not necessarily compete against your coworker or organization. Your strategy should complement it and others so you can make them irrelevant. The thought processes, actions, and skill set that you develop and deploy should make what they do irrelevant. One way this idea is referred to is via "blue ocean strategy," which is defined on the Blue Ocean website as "the simultaneous pursuit of differentiation and low cost to open up a new market space and create new demand. It is about creating and capturing uncontested market space, thereby making the competition irrelevant."[1]

---

1   © Chan Kim & Renée Mauborgne. All rights reserved. https://www.blueoceanstrategy.com/what-is-blue-ocean-strategy/.

List five (5) things that will enable a planning mindset.

1. _____

2. _____

3. _____

4. _____

5. _____

HOW TO CREATE YOUR "BLUE OCEAN."

Think of "market space" as being your position in a company as a woman in leadership. As you use strategic planning and the other guidance we've given you in this workbook, you will be able to differentiate yourself and create a space for yourself in the organization nobody else can fill. By making the competition irrelevant, we don't at all mean demeaning the competition or doing anything that has a negative connotation. We are talking about making them irrelevant because they are quite literally not relevant compared to you and what you have to offer.

TLC EXERCISE

Referring to page 39 of our book, *Teams, Leaders, and Change TLC: Accelerating Women in Leadership*, expound on the bullets as a woman in leadership to determine where you are and where you want to go.

1. _____

2. _____

3. _____

4. _____

5. _____

6. _____

7. _____

Each one of these strategies will open doors to you that may otherwise remain closed and will give you an opportunity to relate to the head (knowledge as you teach), heart (feelings as you relate), and soul (motivations as you walk alongside) of others.

Leverage professional development, knowing that continuous improvement is the key to success.

A major focus of your strategic planning as a woman in leadership should be to complement and add value to your organization. Continuous improvement and learning is one of the enablers that allows you to do just that, while setting yourself apart and making your competition irrelevant. You want to make sure you are doing everything in the most efficient and productive way every single day of the week and on every single component or challenge that you are responsible for.

Continuous improvement and continuous learning occur in collaboration with one another. Continuous improvement speaks to organizations and products, while continuous learning is an individual's response to the modern workplace. With things changing constantly, including leadership strategies, staff, and even the direction of companies, we have to be agile as women professionals.

WHAT DOES PROFESSIONAL DEVELOPMENT INVESTMENT AND KNOWING THAT CONTINUOUS IMPROVEMENT IS THE KEY TO SUCCESS ACTUALLY MEAN?

An investment is the individual planting seed with the expectation of a harvest. When you invest today in your professional development, you will yield results in the future. This is making a strategic choice to set yourself apart from others by obtaining additional training, mentoring, and coaching, to get to where you want to go in your career. Thus, these continuous improvements you make regarding your professional capabilities open doors to new, successful opportunities.

WHY IS IT IMPORTANT?

The investment you make in your professional development presently is vital to how you shine in the marketplace in the future. Failure to make this investment may result in your competition overtaking you. The goal is to become more efficient and more productive. You learn how to collaborate internally and externally by continuously improving, making yourself more relevant and successful.

WHAT DO YOU NEED TO DO?

The SPOT analysis and other tools mentioned earlier in this workbook are valuable resources to shore up and strengthen yourself and your abilities. As a leader, you can also leverage assessments (such as DiSC®) that can help you better understand your leadership style and that of others, so you'll know when to flex to achieve the optimal desired outcome.

To be innovative leaders, we must stay up to date. What is happening in our industry? What can we learn from that to bring additional impact to our companies? A Pew Research Center survey found that 87 percent of workers think it is essential to develop new skills to keep up with the changing workplace.[1] We need to be continuously learning. We need to be implementing continuous improvements.

TLC EXERCISE

Refer to pages 44 – 51 of the TLC book to identify with the ways women made investments in their technical and/or professional development to make a difference in continuous career improvements. Identify how you can invest in yourself both technically and professionally to enhance your leadership capabilities.

1. _____

2. _____

3. _____

4. _____

5. _____

Review the "**AIM HIGHER**" elements discussed on pages 46 – 48 of our book, *Teams, Leaders, and Change TLC: Accelerating Women in Leadership*, and rate yourself (Yes or No) on whether or not you have actually invested in advancing and improving your career. List the things you can do to invest in your technical and professional success.

---

1   https://www.pewresearch.org/internet/2017/05/03/the-future-of-jobs-and-jobs-training/

Element	Element Definition	Rating	Investments Needed
A	Advance		
I	Improve		
M	Marketability		
H	High Demand		
I	Innovative		
G	Genuine		
H	Helpful		
E	Excel		
R	Ready to Act		

Discuss below what, if anything, you consider as your 3 to 5-year strategy for investing in your professional development capabilities. Why this is important to you?

_____

_____

_____

_____

_____

_____

_____

_____

_____

_____

_____

_____

_____

_____

Have an attitude for altitude—and soar!

Through the TLC: Teams, Leaders, and Change Program, we hope we have given you the direction and the tools to not give out, not give in, and not give up. Your attitude will make a difference, and it will give you the altitude to soar as a woman in leadership. If you can see yourself as being impacted by someone else in a way that changes your destiny, then you can find things to be a part of, and identify people you can help, so that someday they will thank you for being a part of their destiny.

We want to take this opportunity to thank you for being part of our destiny by reading this workbook and the coinciding TLC book and participating in our TLC Program—and we are thrilled to be a part of your destiny. Remember, you can do anything that you set your mind to do.

For much of her young life, Dr. Amanda Goodson struggled with self-confidence. In school, her teachers did not think she was as intelligent as the other kids, and she didn't perform well on standardized tests. Still, she made better than average grades in all her courses, even if her teachers didn't recognize it. As a high school student, Amanda took part in a math competition and won eighth place in the entire school, the only girl and African American in the top ten. Yet she was still shocked when her name was called because she never viewed herself as being smart. Everyone had told her she was average, which seeped away at her confidence.

As her senior year neared an end, Amanda realized she needed to decide what she was going to do as an adult. With her father's encouragement, she went to the library to research what professions paid well that might fit with her two interests, math and music. It was clear. Engineers and accountants generally made money, while musicians didn't. So, she thought, engineering it is. She made an appointment with a high school counselor. "Girls are not engineers," she was told, point blank. "Maybe you should go into the military or be a nurse."

That was her first experience with gender bias—and Amanda didn't give in to it. It wasn't that she thought there was anything wrong with being a nurse or in the military. She just knew those weren't the paths for her. So, despite her counselor's advice to not go to a traditional four-year college, she decided she would, starting with *Preface*, a summer pre-engineering program for high school graduates at Tuskegee University. It was there where her instructors first told her she was smart, and it inspired her to apply herself and study like she never had before.

From that moment on, Amanda decided she was not going to be average and that she was going to excel as a young engineering student at Tuskegee—a decision that ultimately landed her with her first post-graduation job at NASA (The National Aeronautics and Space Administration).

As we reach the conclusion of the TLC Program, please answer the following questions.

WHY IS TLC IMPORTANT?

As a change agent, on teams, or as a leader, it is vitally important to utilize the tools provided in the TLC book and workbook to accelerate yourself in your career. Consider your altitude relative to where you want to go. Your attitude will determine how far you soar in your career.

Please revisit the Foreword for the *TLC: Teams, Leaders, and Change: Accelerating Women in Leadership* book, written by Sibongile Sambo, founder and CEO of SRS Aviation. Conduct research on why she started her company and how she allowed her attitude to cause her to soar.

Additionally, read the story about Elijah Cummings beginning on page 53 to determine how his story resonates with you having the right attitude at the right time, for you to make a difference in your career. His attitude allowed him to overcome adversity to excel his career. How will his story change your attitude about becoming a better leader of change in the marketplace?

TLC EXERCISE – CONCLUSION:

What are the top five (5) things that you learned from reading the book and workbook, as well as participating in the TLC Program?

1. _____

2. _____

3. _____

4. _____

5. _____

Discuss three (3) things you will change going forward to create a compelling future for yourself and others?

1. _____

2. _____

3. _____

Review the summary points of each chapter, beginning on page 57 of the *TLC: Teams, Leaders, and Change: Accelerating Women in Leadership* book. List three to five (3 to 5) key action points and give your final thoughts on each chapter.

1. _____

2. _____

3. _____

4. _____

5. _____

Dr. Amanda H. Goodson is a groundbreaking aerospace engineer who soared to become the first woman to hold the Director of Safety and Mission Assurance position out of the Marshall Space Flight Center at NASA. Transformed from a young African American girl who was told by her teacher that she would not amount to much, Dr. Goodson uses her unstoppable "can do" spirit to inspire others to achieve their goals regardless of the obstacles.

Noted nationally for her achievements, Dr. Goodson is the recipient of the Southwest Alliance for Excellence Leadership Award; the Tucson's Woman on the Move Award for Leadership, Achievements, and Continuous Improvement in the Workplace; the Exceptional Service Medal; the Federal Employee Supervisor of the Year Award; and the Director's Commendation for Leadership Excellence in Safety, Quality, and Mission Assurance at NASA.

Dr. Goodson has served as the board of directors' chair for Advancing Minorities Interest in Engineering (AMIE), a national consortium for industry, government, and academia. In addition to serving in a leadership position for a Fortune 500 aerospace company, Dr. Goodson is the senior pastor at Trinity Temple CME Church in Tucson, Arizona.

Dr. Yvette Rice is a results-oriented Executive with Front End of the Business acumen and demonstrated success in developing and executing technical communications strategies that maximize team effectiveness, develop talent, and drive lasting cultural change. Dr. Rice has used her executive leadership and communication skills to direct and oversee Technical Writing teams that develop Win-Win strategies for acquiring contracts with city, state, and federal governments, for businesses, and non-profits nationally and internationally. A published author, Rice utilizes her expertise, influence, and business insight to partner with Sr. Executives of large corporations to produce books, white papers, and prolific articles related to Leadership Development, Mentorship, Coaching, as well as Business Advancement, developing and deploying platforms globally. Serving as a co-pastorship with her husband for a local church congregation, and her 40-year career span has ignited Rice's passion for empowering women in the marketplace with a Biblical twist.

A life-long learner, Rice has a Bachelor of Science degree in petroleum engineering from the University of Alabama in Tuscaloosa and a masters and doctoral degree in theology from the North Carolina College of Theology Satellite Extension Program; Wilmington, North Carolina. She is also a 2021 Graduate of the Jack Welch Management Institute Online MBA Program – Strayer University. Additionally, Rice is a certified Trainer, Coach, and Speaker through the John Maxwell Online University Certification Program.

Odetta Scott, MBA, MSOD, is a certified Six Sigma Black Belt and serves as an Associate Director of Indirect Procurement in a Fortune 100 aerospace and defense company. Scott attended the United States Naval Academy for two years before an illness ended her dreams of becoming an astronaut. Changing those aspirations, Scott chose to help others pursue their dreams of space flight by completing her bachelor's degree in mechanical engineering technology at Texas A&M University. Scott obtained a Master of Business Administration degree from Jackson State University and earned a master's degree in organization development from Pepperdine University.

A valued professional development consultant, Scott spearheads a Leading Inspired Females in Technology recognition and retention sub-team. She also serves in organizations such as Advancing Minorities Interest in Engineering, the Society of Women Engineers, and as a STEM ambassador. An author, advisor, mentor, and lecturer, Scott fuels the development of individuals at all levels while driving transformational cultures in professional and business settings. Scott uses her "each one reach one" mentality to drive herself as a woman and as a leader to fulfill her God-given passion to better herself and others. Odetta was awarded the 2021 Diversity Leadership Award by Career Communications Group, Inc., for promotion and advancement of the diversity journey in her organization, education, small-business development and community activities.

WHO WE ARE

WeTECH Rocks is a Women in Technology consortium with a vision of becoming a global leader in bridging the gap for the advancement of women in technology and other industries in the marketplace. Our mission includes accelerating value delivery, skills development, and strategy execution for leaders and entrepreneurs in Science, Technology, Engineering, and Mathematics (STEM). Our goal is to impart, in women and young ladies who are emerging in business, industry, the community, and in academia, how to become better leaders.

WHAT WE DO

As a catalyst for women in technical careers, as well as other industries, we provide support in ways that build confidence, strengthening them in their respective fields by:

- Developing best practices and solutions for women to secure better jobs and achieve better placement in STEM and in Leadership in the areas they desire.
- Creating opportunities where senior women leaders in the community can come and share ideas and wisdom through mentorship and coaching.
- Facilitating a transfer of knowledge and skills to help young women develop greater competence and confidence.
- Rendering competition irrelevant because of the inimitable skills these women bring to the table.

CORE CAPABILITIES

- Professional and leadership development
- Effective verbal and written communication development
- Presentation skills

- Conflict management
- Leadership acumen
- Personal branding
- Emotional Intelligence
- Self-awareness
- Confidence
- Critical thinking

SPECIALIZING IN THE FOLLOWING AREAS:

- Leadership development for minorities
- Six Sigma methodology expertise
- Data capture and analysis
- Effective communication skills development
- Executive coaching
- Mentoring
- Strategic planning
- Cultural awareness

If you are interested and want more information, you can reach WeTECH Rocks
at wetechrocks@gmail.com.

BOOKS WRITTEN BY OR INCLUDING CONTENT FROM YOUR THREE TLC AUTHORS

Professional and Personal Development

TLC Teams, Leaders, and Change: Accelerating Women in STEM, by Dr. Amanda H. Goodson, Dr. Yvette Rice, and Odetta Scott MBA, MSOD

TLC Teams, Leaders, and Change: Accelerating Women in Leadership, by Dr. Amanda H. Goodson, Dr. Yvette Rice, and Odetta Scott MBA, MSOD

Astronomical Leadership by Dr. Amanda H. Goodson

The Purpose and Power of Mentorship, compiled by Dr. Amanda H. Goodson and Marvin Carolina, Jr.

12 Power Principles for Administrative Professionals by Dr. Amanda H. Goodson

Soar to Your Destiny: 5 Winning Success Strategies by Dr. Amanda H. Goodson

How to Unlock Your Full Potential: 11 Keys to Leader Success by Dr. Amanda H. Goodson, Odetta Scott, and Frederick Cross

Resilient: A Key to Being Brilliant, compiled by Dr. Amanda H. Goodson and Daniel L. Scott, Jr.

Inspirational Books

Women in Leadership: Living Beyond Challenges, compiled by Dr. Amanda H. Goodson Amanda and Dr. Yvette Rice

Phenomenal Prayer: Activating Who You Are by Dr. Amanda H. Goodson

Switch to Holiness Workbook: 12 Actions to be Your Best by Dr. Amanda H. Goodson

Spiritual Intelligence by Dr. Amanda H. Goodson

The Power Behind Your Need is in Your Seed by Dr. Amanda H. Goodson

Financial Healing from the Inside Out by Angela C. Preston and Dr. Amanda H. Goodson

Chosen to Worship: 21 Days of Prayer by Dr. Amanda H. Goodson

Powerful People Follow Christ by Dr. Amanda H. Goodson

Mountain Moving Made Easy by Dr. Yvette Rice

Mountain Moving Made Easy Workbook by Dr. Yvette Rice